George Washington

by Lola M. Schaefer

Consulting Editor:
Gail Saunders-Smith, Ph.D.

Consultant:
Michael C. Quinn, Deputy Director
Mount Vernon Ladies Association

Pebble Books
an imprint of Capstone Press
Mankato, Minnesota

Pebble Books are published by Capstone Press
818 North Willow Street, Mankato, Minnesota 56001
http://www.capstone-press.com

Library of Congress Cataloging-in-Publication Data
Schaefer, Lola M., 1950–
    George Washington/by Lola M. Schaefer.
        p. cm.—(Famous Americans)
    Includes bibliographical references and index.
    Summary: A simple look at the life of the man who led the patriot troops in the Revolutionary
War and later became the first president of the United States.
    ISBN 0-7368-0110-3
    1. Washington, George, 1732–1799—Juvenile literature. 2. Presidents—United States—
Biography—Juvenile literature. [1. Washington, George, 1732–1799. 2. Presidents.] I. Title. II. Series.
E312.66.S33 1999
973.4′1′092—dc21   98-19305
[B]   CIP
                                                                                  AC

Note to Parents and Teachers

This series supports national history standards by providing easy-to-read
biographies of people who had a great impact on history. This book describes
and illustrates the life of George Washington, the first president of the United
States. The photographs support early readers in understanding the text.
Repetition of words and phrases helps early readers learn new words. This
book introduces early readers to vocabulary used in this subject area. The
vocabulary is defined in the Words to Know section. Early readers may need
assistance in reading some words and in using the Table of Contents, Words to
Know, Read More, Internet Sites, and Index/Word List sections of the book.

Table of Contents

George Washington was born in Virginia on February 22, 1732. Virginia was a colony at that time. People in Virginia followed British laws. They were colonists.

George grew up on Ferry Farm. He went to school and learned to read and write. Later, George became a surveyor. A surveyor measures land and makes maps.

George moved to Mount Vernon in 1752. Mount Vernon was a big farm. George first grew tobacco. Then he grew wheat.

10

George joined the Virginia army in 1752. The Virginia army helped Great Britain fight France. The countries fought over land. George helped the Virginia army win land for Great Britain.

George returned to Mount Vernon after the war. He married Martha Custis in 1759. She was a widow who had two children. George loved the children as his own. They all lived at Mount Vernon.

Colonists grew tired of Great Britain's laws. Great Britain would not give the colonists their freedom. The colonists began fighting the British army in 1775. This was the start of the Revolutionary War.

George was commander in chief of the Continental army. He trained men how to be soldiers. He led the soldiers into battles. The Revolutionary War lasted eight years.

The Revolutionary War ended in 1783. The colonies became the United States of America. George returned to Mount Vernon. But he did not stay there long. People wanted George to be president.

20

George became the first president of the United States in 1789. He served his country for eight years. Then George returned to Mount Vernon. He died in 1799. People call George Washington the Father of Our Country.

Words to Know

battle—a fight between two armies

colonist—a person who lives in a colony

colony—land that people from another country have settled

commander in chief—a person who leads an army

freedom—the right to do and say anything

Revolutionary War—the war in which the 13 American colonies won their freedom from England; this war lasted from 1775 to 1783.

surveyor—a person who measures land and makes maps

tobacco—a plant that has leaves used for smoking or chewing

wheat—a grain used for making flour, pasta, and breakfast foods

widow—a woman whose husband has died

Read More

Milton, Joyce. *The Story of George Washington: Quiet Hero.* Famous Lives. Milwaukee: Gareth Stevens Publishers, 1996.

Usel, T. M. *George Washington: A Photo-Illustrated Biography.* Read and Discover Photo-Illustrated Biographies. Mankato, Minn.: Bridgestone Books, 1996.

Woods, Andrew. *Young George Washington: America's First President.* A Troll First-Start Biography. Mahwah, N.J.: Troll Associates, 1992.

Internet Sites

A Brief Biography of George Washington
http://www.mountvernon.org/image/biobrief1.html

George Washington
http://www.history.org/people/bios/biowash2.htm

Historic Mount Vernon
http://www.mountvernon.org/

Index/Word List

Word Count: 270
Early-Intervention Level: 14

Editorial Credits
Michelle L. Norstad, editor; Clay Schotzko/Icon Productions, cover designer;
   Sheri Gosewisch, photo researcher

Photo Credits
Archive Photos, cover, 1, 6, 14, 16, 18, 20
Corbis-Bettmann, 4, 8, 10, 12